CRIMINAL INVESTIGATION

IAN McKENZIE

Wayland

CONTENTS

First published in 1996 by
Wayland (Publishers) Limited
61 Western Road, Hove, East
Sussex BN3 1JD, England
© Copyright 1996 Wayland
(Publishers) Ltd

British Library Cataloguing in
Publication Data
McKenzie, Ian
Criminal Investigation. (Science
Discovery series)
I. Title II. Series
363.25

ISBN 0 7502 1235 7

This book was prepared for
Wayland (Publishers) Limited by
Globe Education
of Nantwich, Cheshire

Concept David Jefferis
Illustrations Peter Bull

Printed and bound by G. Canale
and C.S.p.A., Turin

Acknowledgements
AFP Photo 29, 41l
Apple Computers Ltd 40r
Art Directors 14, 38
Forensic Science Service 24-25, 25

Ian McKenzie/Amina Memon 44
Ian McKenzie/Scotland Yard cover tl, 8b
Image Select/Ann Ronan 7b, 42l
Life File back cover and tr, 7t, 8-9, 20b, 46
Lion Laboratories plc 27
Peter Newark's Historical Pictures 6, 18t,
18b, 19l, 19r, 36
Popperfoto cover bl, 12, 20t, 28, 32, 33t,
33b, 34, 37, 41r, 43
Science Photolibrary cover centre and br,
5, 9b, 12-13, 16, 17, 21, 22, 23, 26, 26-27,
31, 39l, 39r, 40l, 42r, 45
Tony Stone 4-5, 9m, 13, 15, 35
Zefa 46-47

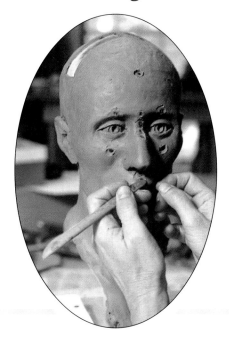

⊛ INTRODUCTION

There is no country in the world that is free from crime. It is unlikely that there ever has been or ever will be such a country. But, equally, no society can exist if people are permitted to rob, or steal from each other, or if they can injure, maim or kill other people with no fear of getting caught. For this reason, all nations and groups within nations have rules about what is not permitted, and these rules are called laws. When laws exist, a society makes arrangements to ensure that the inhabitants keep the peace and obey the laws. The most common method of ensuring tranquility is to set up a body of people who are employed to enforce the law and to bring offenders to justice. Law enforcement officials, usually called the 'police', contain specialist groups of women and men who are given the job of investigating crimes. These people are usually called 'detectives', or perhaps 'crime investigators'.

A detective, however experienced and regardless of rank, is part of a team. The team may consist of many other investigators and will involve scientists and other specialists, all of whom have one aim in mind. In the end, they must have evidence to justify an arrest. They must also have evidence that can be presented to a court so that a jury – or at very least a judge – can understand it.

The investigation team is supported by forensic scientists. Over the years, the work of scientists was incorporated into particular investigative techniques and procedures developed by the police. It is these techniques and procedures that form the basis of what is called the forensic investigation.

▼ A suspect is arrested and taken to the police station for questioning.

'Forensic' is derived from the Latin word *forensis* meaning 'giving the opportunity for debate'. It has come to mean something which is 'of the law'. By that we mean some activity which has at its core an association with things legal, usually in the form of evidence that can be presented to a court. Thus, one definition of forensic science is scientific activity that produces evidence for presentation in court. Forensic science may also be, however, the investigation and development of techniques, tests and information-gathering strategies that will help the detectives and those involved in the prosecution. They must put together a case that will 'stand up in court'.

▼ Blood stains on clothing from a crime scene are analysed in a forensic laboratory. One of the techniques used is genetic fingerprinting. In the picture, genetic fingerprints are the dark bands on the translucent vertical screens.

Forensic scientists come from many different areas of scientific study. These include physics, chemistry, biology, geology, physiology, medicine, dentistry, anthropology and psychology. In addition, forensic science includes some aspects of the study of criminology, particularly those parts which examine the causes of, or seek to explain, criminal behaviour. So, as you can see, the label forensic science is a blanket term covering a wide range of scientific disciplines.

CRIME AND PUNISHMENT

The Hammurabi code of Babylon (eighteenth century BC) was an important ancient law. The Ten Commandments of the Old Testament, the principles of Islam contained in the Qu'ran and the Mosaic law of the third century AD added religious ideas. Roman law dates back to 753 BC, and nowadays in almost every industrialized society, it is possible to trace the source of the current legal and policing systems to those of the ancient Greeks and Romans. In many countries, the legal system includes religious beliefs.

Policing in ancient times was carried out by one of two groups of people, or sometimes by both. In some societies, these were soldiers, perhaps called the Emperor's Guard, or some similar title. In others, the responsibility fell on the people themselves. The word 'police' comes from the Latin word *polites* meaning citizen, carrying the idea that they are of, or about, the people.

▶ This sixteenth-century woodcut shows a woman in a ducking stool. Women suspected of witchcraft might be ducked or thrown into a deep pool of water and held under for a few minutes. If they remained conscious they were accused of being in league with the devil. Witches were usually burned to death by being tied to a stake fixed in the middle of a specially built fire.

After the withdrawal of the Romans from northern Europe in about AD 486, until the end of the Middle Ages around 1500, arbitrary executions were common and many people were declared to be guilty of a crime following a trial by ordeal. One ordeal required that a person accused of theft should lift and carry for five paces a piece of metal that had been heated red-hot. If the burns healed within a given period, the accused was said to be 'not guilty' of the crime. If the wound did not heal (there was virtually no medical knowledge at that time) or if the person refused to lift the red-hot metal, he or she was declared to be guilty – and was almost certainly executed. Gradually, these inhumane practices fell into disuse, but in many countries, as in ancient Rome, the idea had taken root that the people themselves were the source of law and order in their community.

▶ Tracker dogs can follow the trail of a person for many kilometres. Nowadays, German Shepherd (or Alsatian) dogs and Labradors are most commonly used, particularly in urban areas. However, many people still believe that the bloodhound is the best tracker.

▼ Louis Daguerre created the first photographs by using silver-plated sheets of copper. The sheets were made light sensitive by treating them with iodine vapour. They were put in the camera and exposed by removing the lens cap. The pictures were developed using a salt solution.

Some of the techniques now used in forensic science have been used for hundreds of years. People knew that broken pieces fitted together. A broken tip of a knife blade might be found in a wound or lying near a dead body and accurately matched to a broken knife. Then at the very least, the person in possession of the knife had some explaining to do! This procedure is known by forensic scientists as mechanical fit.

Between the sixteenth century and the middle of the nineteenth century, scientists invented, designed and developed the prototypes of many pieces of equipment without which modern forensic science could not exist. In 1673, Anton van Leeuwenhoek (1632–1723), a Dutchman, produced the first effective microscope. In 1728, the German Johann Schultz, noticed that an image of an object could be transferred to a plate coated in silver nitrate and chalk. This idea was later developed in France by Louis Daguerre (1789–1851) when he created the daguerreotype – an early form of photograph.

KEEPING THE PEACE

During the fifteenth and sixteenth centuries, people in Europe started to congregate in cities, and the old practice of people being solely responsible for the peace-keeping of their own locality started to disintegrate. By the start of the seventeenth century, groups of watchmen were assembled in many cities. These people, often elderly and poorly paid, would patrol the streets at night and would attempt to keep the peace.

Later, two methods of policing evolved. The first was based on military organization and practice: a body of men (there were few women in any early policing systems) who were organized as though they were an army. The second was a body, sometimes called civilians in uniform, who were organized to be men of the people rather than an army of occupation. The two styles exist even today: the military style of policing (for example in France, Italy and Pakistan) and the civilian style (for example in Britain and Scandinavia). In some countries the two styles exist side by side.

▲ The caribinieri in Chile wear military style uniforms and could easily be mistaken for army officers.

▶ This mounted policeman, on duty in Chicago, USA, has a more relaxed appearance.

▲ Robert Peel.

In 1829, Robert Peel (1788–1850) the British Home Secretary, was responsible for introducing to London what is usually considered to be the first organized civilian police force – the London Metropolitan Police. Peel deliberately chose uniforms for his officers that had no connection with those of the army.

In some countries there are layers of law enforcement. There may be a government or federal police, a body of officers responsible for a state or province, and more local law enforcement through counties, cities and towns. In the USA, the sheriff is a county-based law enforcement officer. The name is a development of the English 'shire reeve', an official of the monarch who was responsible for the good order of a county.

In 1910, Edmond Locard (1877–1976), a Frenchman and a doctor of medicine as well as a lawyer, was working at the University of Lyons. He proposed that, in all scientific disciplines, the idea that 'every contact leaves a trace' was of particular significance. This idea had profound consequences for the development of forensic science.

At its simplest, this theory suggests that every criminal, usually quite unintentionally, takes something with him or her from the scene of their crime and, at the same time, leaves something of themselves at the scene. If someone is run down by a motor-car, pieces of the car's paintwork may be transferred to the victim's clothing and minute traces of the person's clothing, skin, or body fluids may be transferred to the motor-car. This idea is known as the theory of trace evidence, or sometimes as the exchange principle.

▼ **Evidence collected at the scene of a crime is sealed in sterile plastic bags.**

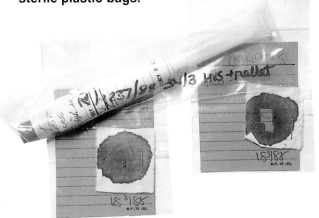

 ## CHAIN OF EVIDENCE

The exchange principle has a number of practical consequences for those collecting evidence from the scene of a crime. Not only will traces of the criminals be left at the scene, but so too will traces of the investigators – unless they are very careful.

In recent years, detectives and scientists have begun to wear overalls when investigating a crime scene. These are made of a special material, often paper, which does not shed fibres and thus contaminate the scene. Investigators place everything they remove into sterile plastic bags. Each bag is numbered and sealed and is only passed on to another person if the person signs for it. This is because, when a trial takes place, the court must be satisfied that the item examined by the forensic scientist is the same as that taken from the scene. This is known as the chain of identification of evidence.

The chain of evidence and the maintenance of forensic integrity are key features of modern crime-scene investigation. Only in films do you see an investigator pick up a gun by sticking a pencil up the barrel, or hold something wrapped in a handkerchief!

IDENTIFYING CRIMINALS

Some people commit crime after crime, undeterred by the threat of imprisonment or even of execution. Early attempts to explain this behaviour assumed that the brains of such people were different. Perhaps their skulls were abnormal, or internal spirits drove them to commit crimes. These ideas were developed by an Italian criminologist, Cesare Lombroso (1836–1909), who studied more than 6,000 criminals in prison. In 1876, Lombroso suggested that physical features were linked to particular types of criminal activity. For instance '... swindlers, bandits and assassins are likely to have a head of exaggerated size', or 'pickpockets, have long hands, a high stature, black hair and scanty beards.'

To provide data to support their arguments, Lombroso and his followers designed and built a range of measuring instruments. The craniograph was a device for accurately measuring and drawing on card the shape of a person's skull. The campimeter was an instrument designed to test Lombroso's idea that some criminal types had poor eyesight. These devices provided the basis for anthropometry – the idea that no two people share the same bodily statistics. Others later built upon this notion, although we now know that Lombroso was mistaken in his ideas.

▼ These are some of Lombroso's criminal types.

'Highwaymen have thick hair and odd-shaped heads.'

'Arsonists have long feet and hands, a small head and weigh less than normal.'

'Swindlers have large jaws, prominent cheekbones, pale faces and are overweight.'

'Pickpockets have long hands, black hair, scanty beards and are tall.'

Alphonse Bertillon (1853–1914) was a junior record clerk with the Sûreté, the French Criminal Investigation Bureau. To identify habitual criminals, hundreds of clerks sifted through hundreds of thousands of verbal descriptions and drawings of people who had been arrested.

Bertillon decided to devise a system of classifying the data and images based on measurements of parts of the body. Within a year of the acceptance of his ideas by his superiors, about 300 prisoners with previous convictions were identified as the culprits in other crimes. Bertillon became famous. Anthropometry was renamed Bertillonage in his honour, and in 1888, he became the Director of the Judicial Identification Service of France.

▲ **Bertillon set up a system of taking measurements of criminals' bodies.**

✷ THE END OF BERTILLONAGE

Bertillon was so convinced of the value of his system that he actively opposed the new science of fingerprinting (or dactylography as it was then known). He reluctantly added fingerprinting to his measurements but did not classify them.

In 1911, the *Mona Lisa*, Leonardo da Vinci's famous portrait, was stolen from the Louvre Museum. Bertillon went to the gallery to supervise the investigation and despite finding a full set of fingermarks on the picture frame, had no way of matching them with his records.

Two years later, a man who had been previously arrested several times in Paris, and from whom Bertillon had taken both measurements and fingerprints, was charged with the crime. He had been arrested returning the painting to Italy.

EXAMINING TEETH

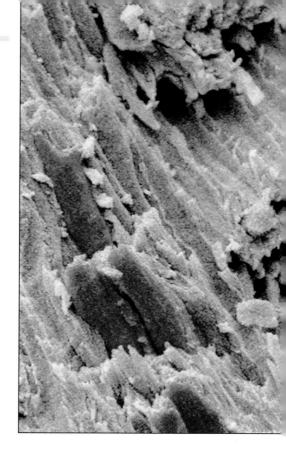

In 1447, the dead body of the French Duke of Burgundy was identified by his missing back teeth. In 1776, the body of General Joseph Warren of the US revolutionary army was dug up and identified by an ivory and silver bridge which replaced a missing tooth. He had been buried by British troops after they had taken Bunker Hill on 17 June 1775 during the American War of Independence (1775–1783).

Forensic dentistry is a science of comparison. If the teeth and jaw of a corpse can be matched to earlier dental records, then the corpse can be identified. Similarly, because teeth both develop and wear in individual ways, a bite mark can be compared with the teeth of a suspect.

▲ Keith Simpson arrives with his camera at a murder scene in Britain on 12 December 1960.

The British pathologist Keith Simpson (1907–1988) developed ways of examining and comparing the teeth of a corpse or skeleton with dental records by using X-rays. His work was further aided by a number of other scientific and technological advances. In 1909, the American physiologist, Thomas Hunt Morgan (1866–1945), established that heredity is passed on through chromosomes. Chromosomes found in the nucleus of human cells are arranged in twenty-three pairs. The twenty-third pair is different depending on whether it belongs to a man or a woman. If the pulp at the core of a tooth is exposed to ultraviolet light and the tooth is from a man, the pulp shines. If it is from a woman, it does not.

In the early 1930s, two German engineers, Ernst Ruska and Max Knoll, built a primitive electron microscope. The idea was developed by the Russian-born Vladimir Zworkin (1889-1992), working in the USA, and today the electron microscope is a critically important tool in the examination of dental and bite-mark evidence. Images and photographs can be magnified up to 150,000 times. Minute variations are clearly visible on the surface of a tooth and in bite marks, allowing very fine comparisons between one surface or imprint, and another.

◄ Human teeth are protected by hard, translucent enamel. Minute marks and variations in the enamel become visible under the electron microscope, allowing detailed comparison of teeth and bite marks.

LEE HARVEY OSWALD

Following the assassination of President John F. Kennedy in Dallas, USA, in 1963, Lee Harvey Oswald, the man arrested for the shooting, was himself murdered. In the late 1970s rumours started to circulate that it was not Oswald who was arrested, but a Soviet spy impersonating Oswald. In 1981, Oswald's body was exhumed and a positive identification made using Oswald's military dental record.

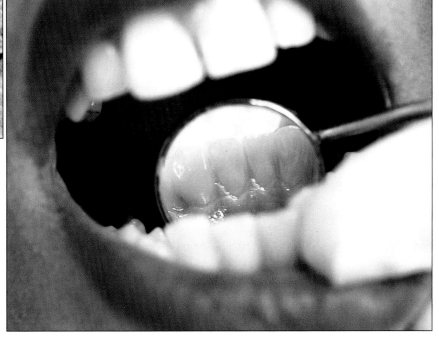

◄ Dentists keep careful notes on each of their patients, regularly recording any loss or damage to their teeth and any treatment carried out.

In 1906, in Britain, the first case went to court in which bite marks left at the scene of a crime by a suspect were used as evidence. One of two men involved in a burglary took a bite out of a piece of cheese, part of which he unwittingly left at the scene of the crime! In 1948, George Gorringe was convicted of the murder of his wife, in part on the evidence of Keith Simpson, who compared a cast of the accused's teeth with a bite mark on the body. This was the first bite-mark evidence to support the conviction of a murderer in Britain. The following year, Keith Simpson was asked to help the investigation of a series of murders. John George Haigh was suspected of murdering, among others, Mrs Durand-Deacon. Her body had disappeared, but eventually, a few pieces of bone and a full set of dentures were discovered at the bottom of a vat of sulphuric acid. The dentures were identified by Mrs Durand-Deacon's dentist. Haigh had been convinced that with no body there could be no trial. However he was later convicted of her murder.

☀ FINGERS AND THUMBS

Fingermarks occur because dirt, blood and many other materials with which the fingers have been in contact are transferred to any surface touched by the fingers. Even a clean hand may be covered in salts, amino acids and other chemical substances which are naturally produced by the skin.

The Italian physiologist Marcello Malpighi (1628–1694) first described the patterns of ridges and pores on the tips of the fingers. It was part of a descriptive study of human skin, and his pioneering work was recognized by the naming of one of the nine layers of human skin as the Malpighian layer.

Although there was other work by Malpighi's contemporaries, it was not until 1823 that Jan Evangalista Purkinje (1787–1869), a Czechoslovakian physiologist, described whorls, ellipses and triangles formed by the lines of the ridges and grooves of the surface of the skin on the fingers.

☀ WILLIAM HERSCHEL

William Herschel (1833–1917), an English civil servant, worked in India for the British colonial government. He suspected that former soldiers, to whom he was paying pensions, were claiming more than once. They were joining the queue, making a mark (an *X* or some such 'signature'), receiving the cash and going straight to the end of the line again. Herschel introduced a procedure in which the men's fingerprints were recorded on both their pay-book and on the receipt form, making fraud impossible.

Herschel also showed that the grooves and ridges of the fingers do not change after the first six months following conception.

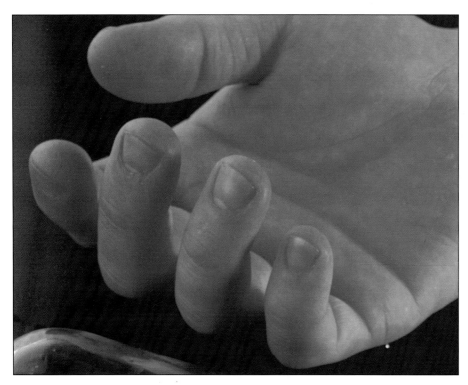

◀ The patterns of ridges on the tips of human fingers were first scientifically examined and described in the seventeenth century by Marcello Malpighi.

▲ At its simplest, a fingerprint is either an arch, a loop or a whorl. (In fact there is a fourth possibility – a composite or compound print – a combination of any one with either or both of the other two.) Statisticians have estimated that 60 per cent of fingerprints are loops, 5 per cent are arches and 35 per cent are whorls or composites.

The first criminological use of fingerprints was made in 1880 by Henry Faulds (1843–1930), a Scottish physiologist, who had been a missionary in Tokyo during the 1870s. Faulds published a paper in which he described 'dactylography', and discussed '... the forever unchangeable finger furrows of important criminals'. Faulds' enthusiasm for dactylography was based upon success in two cases in which he had been involved in Japan. In one, following a break-in, the Tokyo police had arrested a man who fervently denied the crime. At the scene, a hand mark had been found on a white wall. Faulds was able to show that this was not the same as that of the man who was in custody. Although the police refused to accept it, Faulds declared the man's innocence. The police changed their minds however when, a few days later, another man confessed to the crime and was shown to have a palm print that matched the one on the wall.

Superficially, there seem to be millions of different patterns in the grooves, ridges, loops, whorls and arches of the fingertips. Francis Galton (1822–1911), an English scientist, identified basic recurring shapes – the points at which the ridges run together to form a triangle or delta. Galton published his ideas in 1892, describing four basic delta patterns: no delta; delta on the left; delta on the right; and more than one delta. He was encouraged in his efforts by an association with Alphonse Bertillon and through discussion with William Herschel about his experiences in India.

Edward Henry (1859–1931), later to become the director of the Scotland Yard fingerprint branch in Britain, met with Galton and added the final step to the classification process: the identification of the five patterns which are still the core of fingerprint examination to this day. These patterns are: arches, tented arches, radial loops, ulna loops and whorls. The Galton-Henry system went into operation at Scotland Yard in June 1900.

FINGERPRINT RECORDS

One of the first things that Edward Henry did on his appointment to Scotland Yard in 1901 was to set up fingerprint records for all criminals sentenced to more than one month's imprisonment. In 1902, Harry Jackson became the first person to be convicted in Britain because of fingerprint evidence. Harry Jackson was a burglar who left a fingerprint in wet paintwork at the scene of his crime.

In 1911, Thomas Jennings appealed against his conviction for murder in the USA. Jennings had been involved in a burglary that went wrong and had left a perfect impression of four fingers of his left hand at the scene of the crime. The prints were a perfect match to fingerprints of Jennings held in police records. The Supreme Court of Illinois ruled that there was a sound scientific basis for allowing the use of fingerprints in evidence, and that Jennings' death sentence should stand.

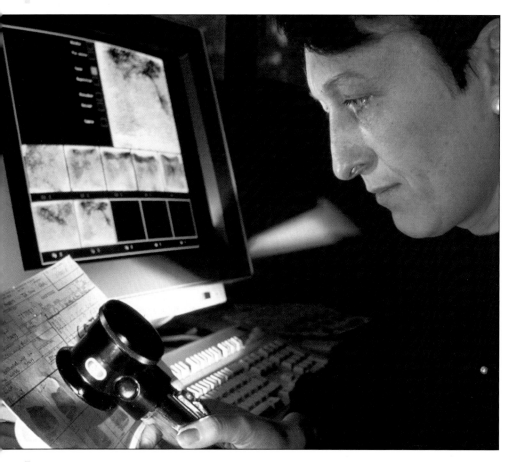

▶ Computer matching of fingerprints allows prints obtained from a crime scene to be digitally matched with prints held in police records. A split screen allows the prints to be viewed side by side, and a comparison program checks both prints, in this case showing they are identical.

◀ Old paper copies of criminals' fingerprints are transferred to a computer system using a hand-held scanner.

Finger-marks at the scene of a crime are exposed in a number of ways, some of which have remained unchanged since they were introduced by Edward Henry in the early part of the twentieth century. The most common are dusting smooth, firm and light-coloured surfaces with fine carbon powder (vegetable black), and dark surfaces with aluminium or lanconide (white) powder. The powders stick to the surface of invisible marks making them visible. Iodine and other chemicals might be used to show up marks on rough or problem surfaces.

In 1960, Theodore Maiman ((1927–) of the Hughes Aircraft Corporation, USA, produced the first laser. Laser light can be used by forensic scientists to flood a room, causing chemicals in any finger-marks to fluoresce. During the 1980s, investigators discovered by accident that the vapour from Super Glue reacts with chemicals in human sweat and produces a white image of finger-marks.

✺ X-RAY FINGERPRINTS

X-rays were first discovered by the German physiologist Wilhelm Conrad Röntgen (1845–1923), in 1895. X-rays are a form of radiation that will pass through soft human tissue but not through other substances, one of which is lead. A British father and son team, William Henry Bragg (1862–1942) and William Lawrence Bragg (1890–1971), shared a Nobel prize in 1915 for discovering that X-rays fired at crystals are scattered in specific patterns which can be captured on photographic plates. In the 1960s, Daniel Graham and Hugh Gray, radiographers at the Glasgow Victoria Infirmary in Scotland, devised a system in which a beam of X-rays is aimed at human skin that has been dusted with lead powder. The electrons released from the lead produce a fingerprint image on X-ray film. This provided a more accurate means of comparing fingerprints.

A fingerprint expert tries to assess how closely fingerprint samples match fingerprints on record. These similarities are called the points of reference. Countries differ over the number of points of reference required to prove beyond any shadow of doubt that a fingerprint left at the scene of a crime matches that of a suspect. In France seventeen are required; in Britain sixteen; Greece, Switzerland and Spain twelve; and India eight to twelve depending on the area. In the USA, following a report by an eminent committee in 1973, a formal minimum standard was abandoned. Prosecutors are now required to convince the jury.

FLINTLOCKS AND EARLY FIREARMS

The inventor of gunpowder and the designer of the first gun probably lived in China in about the third century AD. Basically, almost all firearms are similar in design to early weapons. They have a tube, a projectile and an explosive charge. At first, firearms were loaded by ramming gunpowder down the barrel from the front. A wad of paper or cotton was inserted, followed by a pellet and another wad of paper. To fire the weapon a fuse was lit. Later, flintlocks were fired by striking a flint with metal to make a spark.

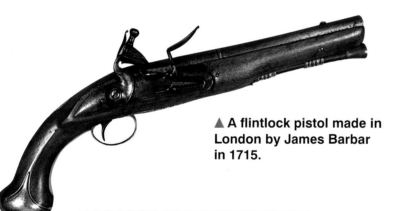

▲ A flintlock pistol made in London by James Barbar in 1715.

▶ A soldier using an early firearm from Jacques de Gheyn's *Manual of Arms*, 1607.

TELLING TALES

In 1794, a British doctor dressing the wound of a Lancashire man who had been shot, found a wad of paper in the wound. The paper had been torn from a ballad sheet and had been used when the gunpowder was loaded down the muzzle of the gun. The remainder of the torn paper was found in the pocket of the main suspect.

In two similar instances, wads of paper were key features in solving murders. The first, in Britain in 1854, involved a piece of the London *Times* newspaper, and the second, in France in 1891, part of the French journal *Lorraine Almanche*.

Early firearms were inaccurate because the inside of their barrels were smooth. Rifling was first used in the sixteenth century. A number of parallel grooves were made which rotated along the inside of the gun barrel. The weapon was loaded from the back with a bullet made of softish material slightly larger in diameter than the barrel. As the bullet travelled down the barrel, the rifling cut into the soft material and made the bullet spin. The spin of the bullet made the aim of the gun more accurate.

The American inventor, Samuel Colt (1814–1862), took out his first patent on a revolver in 1835. He developed the 'six shooter' and also metal cartridges. Cartridges today are usually made of brass, and hold a charge of gunpowder and a bullet. When the trigger is pulled, a pin strikes the bottom of the cartridge, the gunpowder explodes and the bullet sets off down the gun barrel. The first smokeless gunpowder was developed by Alfred Nobel (1833–1896), a Swedish inventor, in 1887. This reduced the smoke cloud produced when a gun was fired.

▲ Samuel Colt was born in the American state of Connecticut and ran away to sea in 1827. He later returned to Connecticut to open a gun factory.

▲ The Colt New Model Army Revolver of 1860 was the principal handgun used during the American Civil War (1861–1865).

As a bullet travels down the barrel, tiny imperfections in the rifling become etched into the bullet. These imperfections are unique to the gun, which means that the rifling marks on a spent cartridge produce a kind of fingerprint linking the cartridge to the gun. During a murder investigation in France in 1889, Alexandre Lacassagne (1844–1921) used this special application of Locard's exchange principle to match a bullet from the murder scene with a gun belonging to the main suspect. Small deformations of the firing pin also become etched into the bottom of the cartridge case. Some modern weapons have a device, called an extractor claw, which removes the spent cartridge case from the weapon and casts it to one side, before another cartridge, complete with bullet and primer, is automatically inserted into the breech. The action of the claw also leaves identifiable marks on the casing.

BALLISTICS

Throughout the nineteenth and twentieth centuries most of the development of firearms and ammunition was in the USA. In 1923, Charles Wait and Phillip Gravell set up the Bureau of Forensic Ballistics (BFB). Later they were joined by Calvin Goddard, a former doctor, who many people regard as the world's first true ballistics expert. Gravell and Goddard developed their own special equipment, most importantly the comparison microscope around 1921. This was basically two separate microscopes joined by an optical bridge allowing two objects to be compared. Modern comparison microscopes allow the two objects to be rotated, moved independently and viewed together on a computer screen.

Also in the early 1920s, another American, John Fisher, invented a device called a helixometer. This was a hollow probe fitted with a light and magnifying lenses. It was used to examine the inside of gun barrels. Today, probes with fibre optic filaments give high-quality images on computer screens.

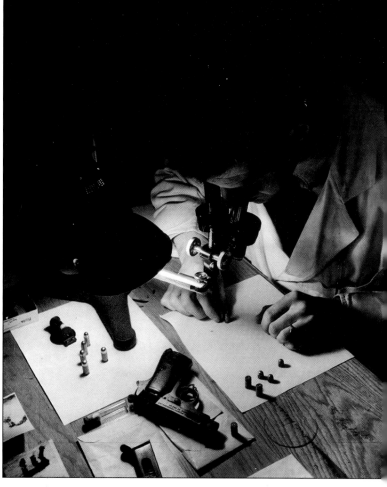

▲ A forensic scientist examines bullets under a comparison microscope to discover whether they were both fired from the same weapon.

▼ Weapons are tested in specially constructed firing ranges. The bullets are collected afterwards and examined in a forensic laboratory.

In the early 1930s Gerald Burrard, an English ballistics expert, devised a way of obtaining test bullets by firing weapons into a water tank. Bullets only travel a few centimetres in water regardless of their previous speed and can easily be recovered from the bottom of the tank. Water tanks are particularly useful today for obtaining test firings from weapons capable of discharging dozens of rounds with one brief squeeze of the trigger, such as machine guns and pistols.

Sometimes forensic ballistics experts need to examine the flight-paths of bullets. The flight of a bullet is known as the trajectory. Trajectories can be calculated in a number of ways. In a relatively enclosed space, provided the position and alignment of the gun is known, a straight line can be drawn along the bullet's projected flight path to the place where the bullet might be found. At simple crime scenes, detectives usually mark supposed and actual trajectories with lengths of string. A small hand-held laser may also be used. However, once bullets enter a human body, they behave in very strange ways, and trajectory predictions are difficult to make with certainty.

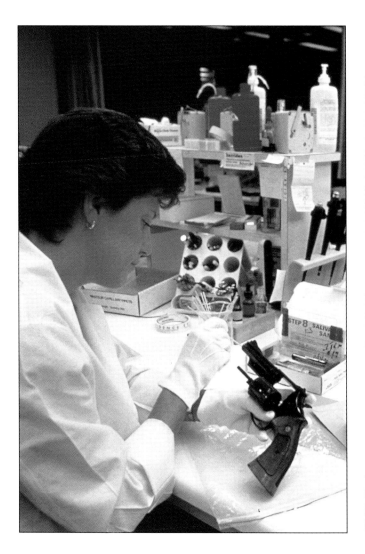

 THE MAGIC BULLET

After the US president, John F. Kennedy, had been assassinated in Dallas in November 1963, there was much discussion about what has come to be known as the magic bullet. The rifle fire that hit Kennedy in the neck passed into the shoulder of Governor Connolly, who was seated in front of him, and appeared to exit though his elbow. Some people have claimed that this trajectory was not possible with the type of rifle and ammunition used. Because of this, it has been suggested that there were two different shots from two different gunmen. After more than thirty years of debate, the magic bullet has still not been explained to everyone's satisfaction.

◀ A forensic scientist examines a handgun for traces of blood at the Federal Bureau of Investigation (FBI) laboratory in Washington, USA.

BLOOD TESTS

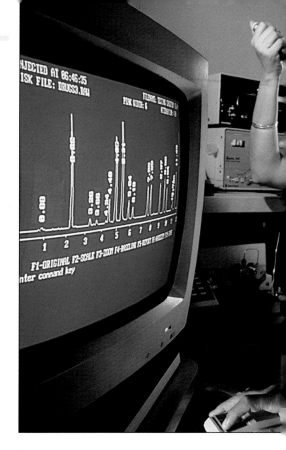

▲ High performance liquid chromatography (HPLC) is used to check substances in blood samples. These appear as peaks on the computer screen.

▶ A minute amount of a liquid sample is sucked into a syringe and injected into the top of the chromatography column. As the liquid passes down the column, it separates into its different components which can be measured.

Ancient Greek physicians believed that human blood was a source of emotion, and we still speak of people being hot-blooded, meaning that they are impetuous and emotional. It was not until 1628 that William Harvey (1578–1657), an English physician, showed that the blood circulates around the body. At the start of the twentieth century, scientists still did not know why the blood from one person often became lumpy when mixed with the blood from another.

In 1901, the Austrian biologist Karl Landsteiner (1868–1943) was able to show that the presence or absence of two factors which he called A and B, and the presence or absence of two types of coagulating agents, which he also called A and B, controlled whether or not blood from two different people would mix.

By 1910 the four main blood groups had been identified: A, B, AB and O. In 1927, Landsteiner and his colleagues defined further secondary groups, and later experiments isolated the rhesus factor, subdividing the main groups into rhesus positive and rhesus negative. Scientists now had a reliable way of classifying people's blood.

Blood Group	Red Cell Antigen A	Red Cell Antigen B	Plasma Antibody A	Plasma Antibody B
A	✔	✘	✘	✔
B	✘	✔	✔	✘
AB	✔	✔	✘	✘
O	✘	✘	✔	✔

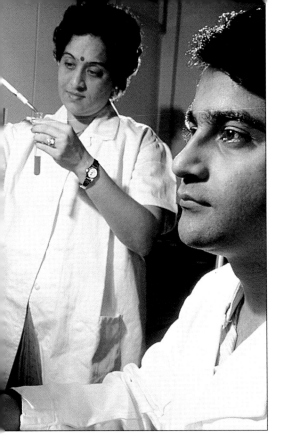

In about 1880 Alexandre Lacassagne suggested that examination of the smearing and staining of blood at a crime scene could provide important trace evidence. John Glaister (1892–1971), a Scottish pathologist, identified five patterns of blood stains (drops, splashes, spurts, smears and trails) in about 1925. In an echo of Locard's exchange principle, he proposed that such patterns could be used to recreate what happened at the scene of a crime. Clearly, it is important to link blood traces to the person they came from.

The development of spectroscopy was an important factor in analysing minute traces of blood and other materials. In 1666, the British scientist, Isaac Newton (1642–1727), had discovered that white light splits into a spectrum of colours when it passes through a prism. In 1859, Gustave Kirchoff (1821–1887), a German physicist, and Robert Bunsen (1811–1899), a German chemist, began work on the idea that when a substance is heated, it gives off a spectrum of light which is typical of the elements contained in the sample. Spectroscopy developed rapidly. Forensic scientists today can rely on fast, accurate analysis using emission spectroscopy and another technique, known as chromatography, in which the components of a substance are identified.

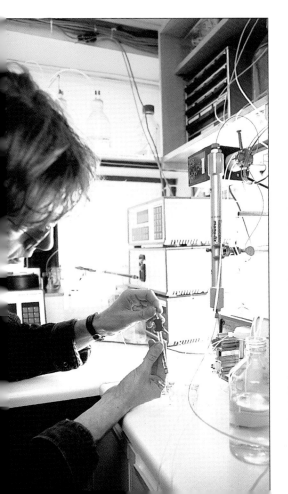

 HOW BLOOD GROUPS MIX

Today we know that blood consists of red blood cells, white blood cells, platelets and plasma. The plasma is a kind of watery fluid in which the cells and platelets float. The surface of red blood cells can contain proteins, called antigens. If your blood group is A then your red cells have the antigen A.

Your white blood cells produce antibodies to fight infections, and they work by homing in on the antigens on the surface of an invading infection. In fact they home in on any antigens that invade your blood. If you are blood group A, you don't make antibodies against your own antigens, but if you are given blood of group B for example, your white cells immediately make antibodies to destroy the antigen B.

Blood group O has no antigens, so in theory anyone can safely be given group O blood, though in practice other factors have to match. If you are blood group AB, you have both A and B antigens. Scientific studies have suggested that about 42 per cent of people are group A, 9 per cent are group B, 46 per cent are group O and only 3 per cent are group AB.

PIECES OF PAPER

Edmond Locard was one of the first forensic scientists to develop expertise in both handwriting analysis and chemical methods of ink analysis. When handwriting is disputed or needs to be identified, experts compare it with a number of 'control' samples. Although forgers may copy the general shape of letters, the 'incidentals' like slant, the way in which words or sentences start and how the letters are connected one with the other, are much more difficult to copy. A comparison is made using a piece of equipment called a comparison projector. In a sense this is much like the comparison microscope, described on page 20. In this case, however, the images are projected so they can be superimposed, one on the other, and the slant, shape, connectors and so on can be directly compared.

▲ The writing on a cheque can be verified by using ultraviolet light to expose any alterations.

Invisible radiation is another useful tool for forensic scientists examining documents. In the 1670s, Hans Christian Huygens (1629–1695), a Dutch physicist, had suggested that light travels in waves. In 1804, the German physicist, Johann Ritter (1776–1810), discovered ultraviolet (UV) light. This is radiation similar to light but with a wavelength beyond the range of human vision. Ultraviolet light allows chemical reactions to take place which otherwise would not occur and can show up things that are invisible to the naked eye. The modern handwriting expert uses ultraviolet light to expose erasures and blemishes in disputed documents.

X-rays have an even shorter wavelength than ultraviolet light. Using the technique for producing X-ray images of fingerprints (see page 17), Daniel Graham and Hugh Gray developed a procedure known as electron-autography, which allows X-ray images to be made of fingerprints and impressed writing under stamps and inside envelopes.

If there is a piece of paper underneath one that is being written on, impressions of the handwriting are left on the lower piece of paper. Indented impressions can be very useful in an investigation when pages have been torn from account books or personal diaries. The simplest method of showing the impressed writing is to shine a light across the surface of the paper and to photograph the result.

In the late 1970s, scientists realized that impressions left on a piece of paper alter the electrical qualities of the surface of the paper. Using this idea, Bob Freeman (1946–) and Doug Foster (1946–) working in Britain at the London School of Printing in 1978, developed the Electro-Static Detection Apparatus (ESDA). A piece of paper that has been electrostatically charged is sprinkled with a mixture of photocopy toner (carbon) and fine glass beads. Any impressed writing on the paper stands out because the carbon sticks to it. Legibility depends on the depth of the impression. Even where there is no visible impression, handwriting has been exposed using this method.

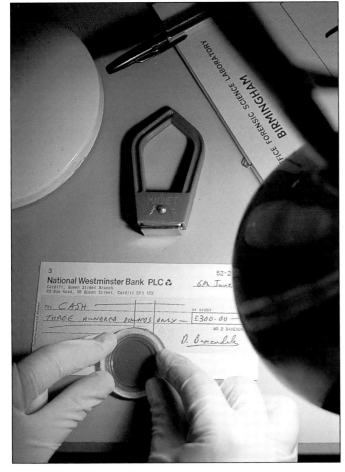

◀ A forensic scientist examines the account number on a bank cheque to make sure it is genuine.

 ## REVEALING BLANK PAGES

William Podmore was found guilty of the murder of Vivian Messiter in Britain in 1929. The conviction was based in part on photographic evidence that showed an impression of Podmore's handwriting on the blank page of a receipt book from which the nine previous pages had been torn. Podmore, an employee of Messiter, had been preparing false receipts for items not sold and claiming the commission. When Messiter discovered the fraud, Podmore killed him.

ALCOHOL AND OTHER POISONS

▲ Attempts have been made, with some success, to analyse the blood of mummies, which have been entombed for thousands of years.

Occasionally, people use poisons to kill others. In such cases, the job of the forensic scientist is to analyse the blood, body fluids and tissue of the victim to find out the exact cause of death. As long ago as 1814, in his work *Traité de Poisons*, Mathieu Orfila (1778–1853), a Spanish chemist, published a system for classifying poisons. Later, in 1836, Alfred Taylor expanded this classification, and developed techniques of drug and poison identification. In the same year, James Marsh developed a test for identifying the poison, arsenic, in human tissue.

Dozens of tests and procedures now exist to identify particular drugs and toxins. Some procedures, such as mass spectrometry, are incredibly sensitive. The first mass spectrometer was built by the British scientist, Francis Aston (1877–1945), who used it to research the isotopic structure of elements for which he was awarded a Nobel prize in 1922. The machine analyses components by their mass, and was soon adapted to analyse minute samples of drugs and blood. In nearly all countries in the world, it is a crime to sell or manufacture certain kinds of drugs and other dangerous substances without a licence. In many places unlawful possession of drugs is severely punished – sometimes by execution. Sensitive, reliable tests are of vital importance.

▶ A scientist injecting a sample into a mass spectrometer. The components in the sample appear as peaks on the computer screen.

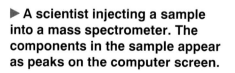

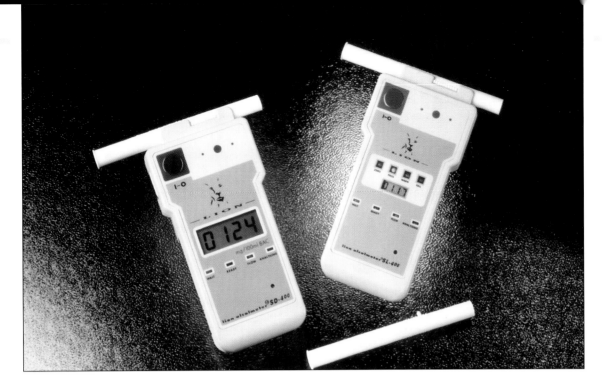

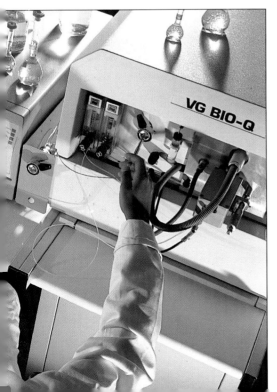

▲ The Lion Alcolmeter 400 series, produced by Lion Laboratories in Wales, is one of the latest sophisticated breath-alcohol measuring devices.

Alcohol is another dangerous substance. Consumed in large quantities it is poisonous and can cause death, but even quite small amounts impair the senses and affect behaviour. In many countries, driving a vehicle after drinking alcohol is a crime. In Britain more than 80 milligrammes of alcohol in 100 millilitres of blood will result in a conviction. In some places, such as the Scandinavian countries and Japan, any alcohol at all found in the bloodstream whilst in charge of a motor vehicle, will result in a conviction.

The amount of alcohol is usually measured in the breath, but may be measured by an analysis of the blood. In the past, drink-drivers were asked to blow down a glass tube containing a crystalline chemical which turned from yellow to green when there was alcohol in the breath. If the green tinge passed beyond a critical mark on the tube, the person would be arrested. Today the police are more likely to use an instrument such as a Lion Alcolmeter. This contains a fuel cell which converts chemical energy into an electrical charge. Alcohol in the breath is the energy source and the electrical current lights either a pass or a fail light.

The Intoximeter, first patented in the USA in the 1980s, is a much larger and more sophisticated machine. It produces a very accurate analysis of the alcohol content of the breath.

Blood samples are analysed for alcohol content using mass spectrometry.

⬤ EXAMINING BONES

Records show that physicians in Alexandria in the third century BC dissected corpses in their efforts to understand disease. In 1284, a book called the *Hsi Yuan Lu* was published in China. It included, amongst other things, descriptions of corpses that had died through drowning and strangulation. The book also contained details of the injuries, including bone injuries, likely to be caused by particular types of weapons.

► In August 1984, a man's body was found in a peat bog in Cheshire, Britain. Scientists were able to show that the man died about 2,500 years ago, and was strangled with a horsehair cord, the remnants of which were still around his neck.

In 1957, two American pathologists, Thomas McKern and Thomas Stewart, identified the stages through which the skeleton passes as a human male ages. This knowledge is the basis for identification of corpses and skeletal remains. In the 1970s, the American Board of Forensic Anthropology proposed a series of procedures which aim to answer a list of questions. Firstly, whether the bones are human or animal. If they are human, how long it is since the person died. Whether the person was male or female and how old he or she was when they died. Finally the height and build of the person, and his or her ethnic origins. Forensic anthropologists might try to discover the existence of illnesses and disorders that might have affected the structure of the bones, such as cancers or an unbalanced diet. They will also look for wounds, fractures or operations.

The age of a person at death can never be more than a guess if only the bones are left, but some accuracy is possible. The teeth of a person under twenty-five years of age can be a positive guide. Changes in bone structure, particularly bone diseases and disorders such as arthritis, may also be a guide to age, as will an examination of the main arteries, if they still exist, because these degenerate with age. The skull can be a good guide because the plates of bone that make up the cranium move together at a known, if slightly variable, rate.

Establishing the sex of the person is not so difficult. Not only are the bones of the pelvis slightly different in males and females but also there are slight differences in the shape of the skull. In males for example, there is a tendency for the bony ridge above the eyes (the supra-orbital ridge) to be more prominent than in females. Similarly there are differences in the back of the skull (the nuchal crest).

▶ On 9 September 1991 a German couple, hiking in Austria, found a human body poking out of the ice of a glacier. The body had been preserved in the ice for more than 5,000 years.

▼ Scientists were able to show that the body was a man aged between 25 and 30 years, about 1.6 metres tall and weighing around 50 kilogrammes. They were able to reconstruct the way the Iceman may have looked.

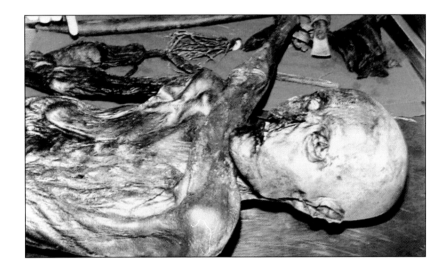

The height of the person can be accurately estimated (to within plus or minus 25 millimetres) by reference to known information about the relationship of physical height to the length of the long leg bones – the femur and the tibia. These data can also provide some information about the gender of the corpse.

Anthropometric measurements can be used to distinguish one ethnic group from another, as can the shape of the skull, the layout of the teeth and the shape of the face.

FROM SKULL TO FACE

During the 1920s Mikhail Gerasimov, a Russian palaeontologist, found a way to assess the thickness of the muscle, flesh, and skin to be expected at any point over the whole of the skull. Using data gathered from the study of the heads of corpses made available to the Third Medical University College in Moscow, Gerasimov studied the relationship between the skull, and the muscles, fibres and tendons that connect one to the other and to the skin covering the head and face. Between 1927 and 1930, Gerasimov used his procedure to reconstruct the facial appearance of the fossilized remains of early humans.

Gerasimov's system was developed and refined in Britain in the 1980s by Richard Neave in the Department of Anatomy at Manchester University Medical School. In 1990, after the discovery of an unidentified female body, a skull-cast was sent to him for reconstruction. The remains arrived in Manchester as 'Little Miss Nobody'. After Richard Neave had worked on her skull-cast, she was identified as Karen Price and two men were later convicted of her murder.

▼ The stages used to reconstruct the face of the Iceman whose body was found in an Austrian glacier in 1991 (*see also* page 29).

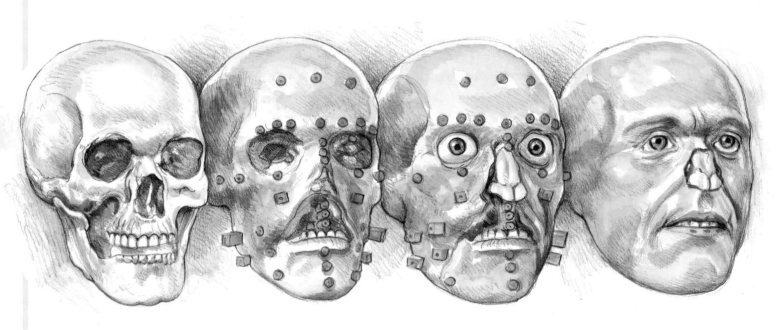

GERASIMOV'S METHOD

Gerasimov's system is deceptively simple. First a cast of the skull is made and the eye sockets are filled with false eye-balls. Then a series of very small holes are drilled at precise positions at various points on the skull-cast. Small pieces of wood are inserted into the holes, the tops of the sticks matching precisely data showing the expected depth of body tissue at that point.

Layers of modelling clay are placed over the skull-cast to the exact height of the sticks. Modelling begins with the jaw and the neck, and is followed by the cheeks, the temples, the mouth and the eyes. The shape of a person's nose is determined by cartilage, which decomposes rapidly, so there is some guesswork over the reconstruction of the nose. On the other hand, much depends upon the expertise of the specialist who uses both the skills of an artist and those of an anthropologist.

As layer after layer of material is built into the model, and skin is added in the form of thin strips, the image appears of a person, perhaps long dead. Some additional guesswork may be necessary with things like the ears and the hair. But in the end there is a face that shows how the dead person might have looked. Many identifications have been made on the basis of such reconstructions.

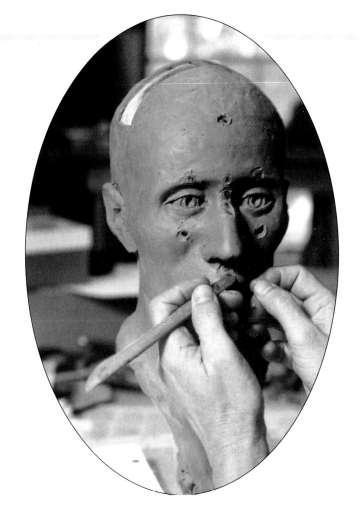

▲ A sculptor works on the finer details of a model head of an unidentified person.

In 1991, a team of anthropologists and physicians working at the Medical Physics Department of University College Hospital, in London, Britain, announced a new technique – laser facial reconstruction. The procedure, developed by Robin Richards and his colleagues, was based on equipment used to predict the outcome of facial surgery. In its forensic science application, a skull (or skull-cast) is put on a rotating plinth. A low-power laser beam is reflected off into a video camera linked to a computer. The computer contains information about skull and tissue shapes, and it creates a mathematical model of the facial appearance of the unidentified person. On the output side of the computer is a machine that cuts a three-dimensional model of the face and head in hard polystyrene foam. Final touches – including perhaps the nose, ears and hair – are added by a sculptor.

IDENTIFYING THE SUSPECT

In the 1940s, Hugh McDonald was the head of the civilian division of the Los Angeles Police Department in California, USA. He was dispatched to Europe to track down a number of criminals, and because he found that the descriptions given by people were both vague and incomplete, he started making rough sketches of the suspects. To save time he drew some of the facial features, such as eyes, noses and face shapes, on transparent sheets and invited people to select those that most accurately matched the person they were seeking to describe.

Later, after considerable consultation, McDonald developed the first Identikit field pack. This consisted of coded and numbered drawings of single facial features, reproduced on transparent sheets. The drawings included eyes, noses, lips, chins, moustaches and beards, but did not include ears, since McDonald believed that '... victims of crime, especially crimes of violence ... never see ... ears properly.'

One of the advantages of McDonald's system, in the days before the fax machine was invented, was that the various features were identified by codes which could be telephoned to an office thousands of kilometres away. Using the codes, the picture could be recreated with ease.

▼ In August 1981, this robbery in Indiana, USA, was photographed by the bank's security camera. Despite the picture, the robber was still unidentified a month later.

In the late 1930s, whilst Jacques Penry (1904–1987) was selecting the photographs for a book he had written called *Character from the Face*, he had the idea of compiling a photographic library of noses, eyes, chins and so on. These could then be used as a resource to produce a photograph of a person. Known as Penry Facial Identification Technique (and later as Photo-FIT), Penry's system superseded Identikit in 1971.

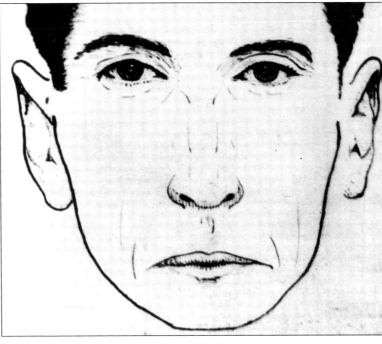

▲ Pictures of suspects, made up from descriptions provided by witnesses, are issued to the newspapers by the police.

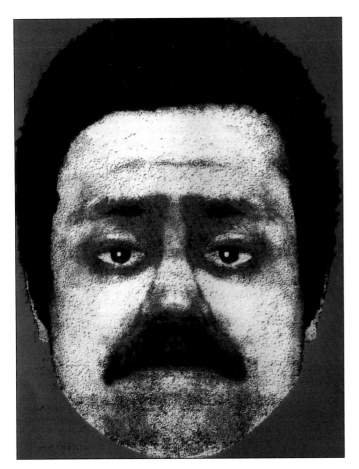

◀ An electronically generated picture of an unidentified man whose body was found on a railway embankment near Leeds in Britain, in March 1995. Electronically generated images provide a more realistic picture, although there is still room for improvement in the technique.

During the 1980s and the 1990s Video fit was developed. This is a procedure not unlike Photo-FIT, except the selection of facial characteristics is made into computer-generated images which can be subtlely adjusted. Adjustments take account of minute observations and witness perceptions. Images are also produced with depth, colour and texture, thus adding to their realism. Similarly, the electronic enhancement of video film taken by security cameras is becoming more commonplace, but it still needs refinement.

✺ QUESTIONING

In the seventeenth century René Descartes (1596–1650), a French philosopher and physiologist, wrote the first scientific reports about automatic behaviour in the human body, such as breathing, heart beat and so on. As part of his work, Descartes observed that there are certain reflex actions of the body. One typical reflex is blinking when a puff of air is directed into your eyes. In the eighteenth century Luigi Galvani (1737–1798), an Italian physiologist, showed that messages are carried from the brain to the muscles as electric currents running along the nerves. Although this current is weak, it is measurable. Galvani also noticed that when people are under stress, the electrical conductivity of the skin changes. This is known as the galvanic skin response (GSR).

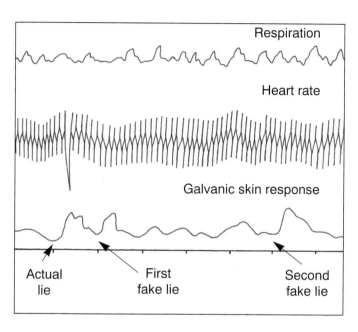

▲ A print-out from a polygraph machine believed by some people to be useful to detect when people are lying.

▲ René Descartes was interested in many ideas besides the reflex actions of the human body.

These observations helped people understand the autonomic nervous system, which is a part of the larger central nervous system of human beings. Some believe that changes in the autonomic nervous system occur when people tell lies. The polygraph is a device that measures changes which occur in GSR, heart rate, breathing patterns and so on. The machine produces a documentary record of these changes when the answer to a question is given.

Unfortunately, there are many, many ways of beating the machine and many psychologists believe that the evidence of lying is little better than guesswork. On the other hand, people who believe that the machine can detect lies and are frightened by it, do react when they tell lies. Some countries allow polygraph evidence to be given in court; many do not.

◀ Psychologists are trying to find reliable ways of helping people to recall events in the past. The techniques would be useful when investigating a crime to help witnesses remember things they have seen or heard.

Günter Köhenken in Germany, and Ray Bull and Amina Memon in Britain, are currently conducting psychological research into ways in which witnesses may be helped to remember what they saw and heard at the scene of a crime.

In Florida and California in the USA, psychologists Ron Fisher and Ed Giesleman, throughout the 1980s and 1990s, have worked on a development known as the cognitive interview. Despite its rather strange name, this is a series of techniques which people can use to remember events they think they have forgotten. For example, a witness says that at a bank robbery she or he heard one of the robbers say the name of an accomplice, but the person cannot remember that name. One technique is to ask the witness to mentally run through the alphabet letter by letter. Sometimes, this triggers the memory.

Smells are very strong cues to accessing memories, so another technique is to encourage the person to think about any smells they might have sensed at the scene. People might also recall sounds, think about what the incident looked like from another position in the room, or try to remember things in reverse order. These and a number of other devices improve the accurate recall of incidents by as much as 40 per cent or more.

CRIMINAL MINDS

Many years ago investigators realized that some criminals had a systematic way of carrying out their crimes. Edward Henry in Britain, and Alphonse Bertillon in France, encouraged their staff to keep records of criminal methods. To this day, major police organizations around the world usually have a methods index in their criminal records office. This index helps identify criminals on the basis of their method of working.

Criminals, who repeat similar types of offences time and time again, are called serial criminals. The most serious of these is the serial murderer. Today, police usually ask psychologists and psychiatrists to help them build a verbal picture of the sort of person they are looking for. In the 1940s, during the Second World War (1939–1945), William Langer, an American psychiatrist, produced a profile of Adolf Hitler, the German leader.

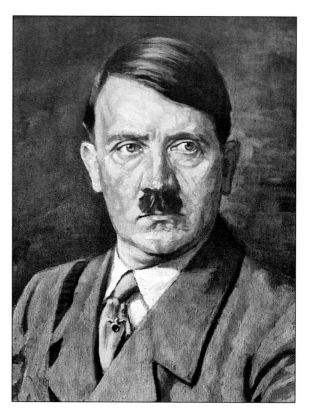

▲ William Langer examined films, documents, and other records of Adolf Hitler. He discussed his subject with people who had met him. He was able to advise Allied commanders that Hitler was not only mentally unstable but also that he would probably kill himself if he lost the war. When Berlin was occupied, Hitler committed suicide. His badly burned body was identified through his dental records.

In 1957, James Brussell, an American psychiatrist, created a profile of a man known as the Mad Bomber, who for sixteen years had waged a terror campaign against the Consolidated Edison Company in New York. Brussell's profile pinpointed Mad Bomber as a single man between the ages of forty and fifty, unsociable but not anti-social, a skilled mechanic and a high-school graduate. When George Metsky was arrested, these and other suggestions in the profile were found to be true. Brussell also created a profile for the Boston Strangler – Albert de Salvo – who was arrested in 1964. Between 1962 and 1963, de Salvo had killed eleven women. Among other things found to be accurate in the profile, Brussell predicted that the offender would be around thirty years of age and Spanish or Italian.

Following the success of Brussell's work, the FBI Behavioural Science Unit, was set up in the 1970s. Now known as the Violent Criminal Apprehension Program, it is a group of FBI agents and behavioural scientists who have compiled a large computerized database of serial criminals and their crimes. This database is available to police forces throughout the world.

The approach to profiling typical of Brussell and of many American profilers, involves matching the symptoms of a known psychological disorder to the crimes and then constructing the profile on the basis of what is known about people who suffer from such disorders.

◀ As well as providing the police with verbal descriptions of serial killers, profiles are often employed when hostages are taken. Profiles assess the behaviour of the criminals and their hostages, and make predictions about the behaviour of both if the police launch an attack.

Another method of profiling is known as the crime scene analysis approach. This is a variation of Locard's trace element approach to forensic science. David Canter (1944–) of Liverpool University, Britain, believes that everything that happens (or sometimes does not happen) at the scene of a crime is of significance in building a profile. Each tiny piece of evidence, both from the crime scene and from witnesses or victims, is of value and can be subjected to rigorous examination, often using computerized plotting techniques. Canter also believes that a serial criminal repeats strategies that have been successful, and changes strategies that have not worked well in predictable ways.

GENETIC FINGERPRINTS

Gregor Johann Mendel (1822–1884), an Austrian monk, spent his lifetime working in the monastery gardens growing peas. Mendel was interested in the ways in which one variety of pea plant, fertilized by another, produced a new variety which had elements in common with each of its parent plants. This process is now known as cross-breeding. In 1865, Mendel published a paper on his studies in cross-breeding dwarf and giant peas. In 1900, three botanists working separately rediscovered Mendel's laws, and in 1909 the American zoologist, Thomas Hunt Morgan (1886–1945), continued the work with fruit flies. In 1930 Morgan received a Nobel prize for establishing that heredity is passed on through the chromosomes. This is one of the basic ideas of genetics.

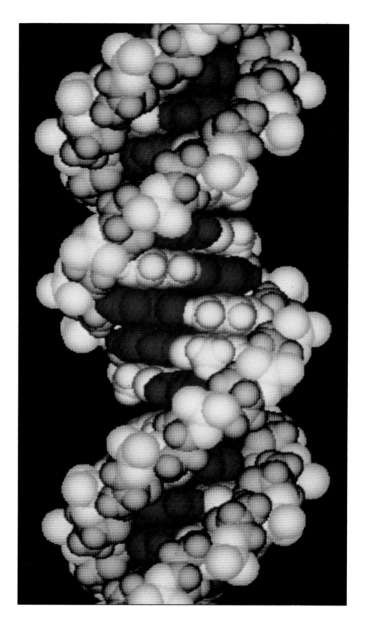

▶ The basic genetic material found in cells is known as DNA. We now know that the DNA molecule has two strands wound round each other and connected at regular intervals.

In 1962 James Watson (1928–), an American, and Francis Crick (1916–) an Englishman, shared a Nobel prize for their work in Cambridge, England, in discovering the structure of deoxyribonucleic acid, or DNA. DNA is contained within the billions of cells that make up the human body. It is a code that is unique to each of us and that also allows us to pass on some of our characteristics to our children.

The techniques of DNA profiling were developed in 1984 by Alec Jeffreys of the Lister Institute at Leicester University in Britain. Jeffreys discovered that DNA can be extracted from the blood and cut up using chemicals taken from certain types of bacteria, which are part of the body's natural defence system. If the DNA sample is placed in a special gel and an electric current is applied, the current causes each of the DNA fragments to move through the gel. The presence and position of each fragment of the DNA sample on the gel are the unique genetic fingerprint of its donor.

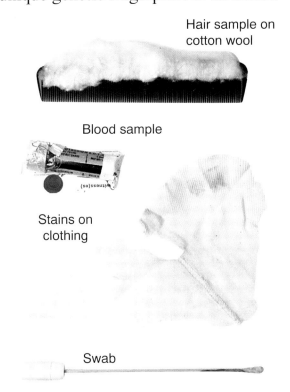

Hair sample on cotton wool

Blood sample

Stains on clothing

Swab

▲ At the forensic laboratory, details of genetic fingerprints are entered into a computer database. This aids identification and cross-matching.

◄ At the scene of a crime, scientists collect evidence from which genetic fingerprints of the criminals can be produced, such as hair, dried blood or sweat stains. A doctor may take swabs of body fluids from rape and assault victims.

Although some people may share one or two DNA similarities, it has been estimated that only two people in 10 billion have identical complete DNA patterns (identical twins are excluded from this calculation as their DNA will be almost identical). Since calculations suggest that the population of the world is about 5 billion, it is assumed for most practical purposes that a person's genetic fingerprint is unique. Comparison of a DNA sample taken from the scene of a crime with that supplied by a suspect is considered valuable evidence of guilt or innocence. Jeffreys' first application of the technique (in 1983) showed that a man, suspected of two murders, one of which he had confessed to, was innocent of both.

DATABANKS

In 1833, Charles Babbage (1792–1871), who had been Professor of Mathematics at Cambridge University, in Britain, made what is usually looked on as the world's first computer. The machine, called the difference engine, was made from very carefully machined brass parts. There was no understanding of electronics at that time and it was not until 1941 that Konrad Zuse, a German, produced a device which worked on the basis of a program, stored within the machine.

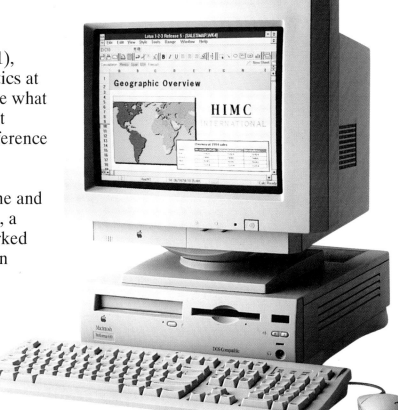

▲ The Macintosh Performa 630CD computer (with a 500 MB internal hard disc and up to 52 MB of random access memory) is far more powerful than the first valve-driven computers, and occupies a fraction of the space.

▲ This false-colour picture, taken by an electron microscope, shows part of the integrated circuit on a silicon chip. The colours relate to different electronic pathways on the surface of the chip. Each indentation on a blue pathway is a single transistor memory cell. At this size, the magnification is about 3,000 times the original.

Early electronic computers were huge, sometimes filling a series of rooms. In 1946, a team of American electronics experts built a machine known as ENIAC. It contained 18,000 electronic valves and filled a large room. In 1948, three American scientists, William Shockley (1910–1989), John Bardeen and Walter Brattain designed the first transistor (a kind of miniature valve). Later, in 1959, integrated circuits on silicon chips were developed by a team of American scientists. These contain many transistors on small wafers of silicon. Even the simpler modern computers, based on silicon chip technology, are more powerful than the early valve-based machines.

► When a bomb exploded on an American passenger aircraft over Lockerbie, Scotland, on 22 December 1988, more than 300 people were killed. The British police collected, numbered, listed and bagged all the pieces of wreckage. This was the beginning of a major international investigation to identify and bring to justice those responsible. Airline security procedures throughout the world were tightened up after investigators discovered how the bomb was hidden on the plane.

◄ On 14 November 1991, Abdel Bassett Ali Al-Megrahi, seen here entering the Supreme Court in Tripoli, Libya, was one of two Libyans charged with the bombing of Pan Am Flight 103.

One major feature of modern law enforcement and crime investigation is the growing need for computerized data to be available to police officers and their support staff, both on a local and on a worldwide basis. Local in-force computer systems are very common and information about crime, criminals and so on can be rapidly passed from place to place. There is a growing number of international agreements which are not restricted by national borders. In Europe, for example, the Schengen Information System (named after the small city in which the agreement was signed) and which currently only involves a handful of countries, is providing the basis for a fully integrated European information system on crime. Most countries in the world have similar systems.

There is, however, nothing new about the sharing of crime and investigation information between nations. For more than fifty years the Interpol (International Police) organization, which has its headquarters in Paris, France, has acted as a coordinating body for international crime investigations. Contrary to popular belief, Interpol does not investigate crime, it merely acts as the channel through which information is passed. It seems highly likely, however, that an international investigative body will gradually develop to counteract crime on a worldwide basis.

TIMELINE OF ADVANCE

Here are some of the people, discoveries, inventions and improvements that have helped shape methods of criminal investigation used today.

Ancient Babylon The Hammurabi code was an important law in ancient Babylon (eighteenth century BC). It was very harsh. If one man accused another of murder but could not prove it, the accuser was executed.

Roman law Roman law (753 BC–AD 235) was very precise and often written down. The first law book was published in about 200 BC.

Mosaic law This was law based upon religious doctrine, including the Ten Commandments about 1100 BC–AD 300. It later developed into the Torah, the Mishna and the Gemara. Much of the law was administered by rabbis.

Middle Ages In the period 1000–1500, legal systems were largely destroyed. Punishments and trials were harsh and unreasonable.

Marcello Malpighi An Italian physiologist (1628–1694) who noticed the patterns on the tips of human fingers.

Anton van Leeuwenhoek A Dutch scientist (1632–1723) who built the first effective microscope in 1670.

Luigi Galvani An Italian physiologist (1737–1798) who established that the transmission of information through the nervous system is electrical. This observation is the basis for lie-detection equipment.

▲ **Luigi Galvani.**

Mathieu Orfila A Spanish chemist (1778–1853) who published a system for classifying poisons in 1814. It is still the basis of forensic toxicology.

Jan Evangelista Purkinje A Czechoslovakian physiologist (1787–1869) who described the ridges, and grooves of the surface of the skin of the fingers.

Robert Peel A British politician (1788–1850) who on 29 September, 1829, was responsible for the first fully functional, civilian police: the London Metropolitan Police.

▲ **Anton van Leeuwenhoek**

Francis Galton An English scientist (1822–1911) who described the four basic 'delta' patterns of fingerprints.

Cesare Lombroso An Italian criminologist (1836–1909) who in 1876 proposed that the physical features of people indicated particular types of criminal activity. He also suggested that most criminals, because their physical appearance determined their behaviour, were incapable of avoiding a life of crime.

William Herschel An English civil servant (1833–1917) who developed a fingerprinting system to prevent fraud by Indian Army soldiers.

Thomas Hunt Morgan An American physiologist (1886–1945) who in 1909 established that heredity is passed on through the chromosomes, confirming one of the basic ideas of genetics.

Henry Faulds A Scottish physiologist (1843–1930) who in the 1870s published a paper describing 'dactylography', an early form of fingerprinting.

Alexandre Lacassagne A French criminologist (1844–1921) who was the father of forensic science. Among his numerous discoveries he pointed out that 'rifling' inside a gun's barrel leaves unique marks on the bullets fired from the gun. He also suggested that blood stains and blood marks at the scene of a crime leave evidence of what happened during the crime.

Wilhelm Conrad Röntgen A German physicist (1845-1923) who discovered X-rays. X-rays are now used in forensic dentistry, in fingerprint examination and in the examination of documents.

Alphonse Bertillon A French criminologist (1853–1914) who developed a system to identify criminals from their body measurements. This became known as 'Bertillonage'.

Edward Henry An English criminologist (1859–1931) who finalized the classification of fingerprints. In 1901 he became director of the fingerprint branch at Scotland Yard in London.

Carl Landsteiner An Austrian biologist (1868–1943) who in 1901 identified the antigens (A and B), enabling the first blood-typing to take place.

▲ **Alexandre Lacassagne**

Edmond Locard A French doctor and lawyer (1877–1976) who had been a student of Alexandre Lacassagne at the University of Lyons. In 1910 he published his ideas about the exchange principle.

Vladimir Zworkin A Russian physicist (1889-1992) who designed and developed the scanning electron microscope, which enabled images to be magnified by up to 150,000 times.

Jacques Penry A photographer (1904–1987) who developed a method that allowed witnesses to put together photographs of facial features to create the full face. Now called Photo-FIT, it replaced the line drawings used by Identikit.

Keith Simpson A British forensic pathologist (1907–1988) who was responsible for many developments of forensic science, including those of forensic odontology and pathology. He was involved in many famous British criminal cases.

William Shockley An American physicist (1910–1989) who, with John Bardeen and Walter Brattain, developed the first transistor in 1948. This small device replaced bulky electronic valves, allowing rapid developments in electronic engineering and computer technology.

Theodore Maiman An American physicist (1927–) who designed the first laser. Laser light, which is concentrated, pure light, can be used to show up fingerprints. It has many other commercial applications.

James Watson An American scientist (1928–) who, with his English colleague **Francis Crick** (1916–), was responsible for the identification and description of the structure of DNA. This work underpinned the development of genetic fingerprinting in 1984.

Robert Freeman A British engineer (1946–) who, with **Douglas Foster** (1946–), designed the The Electro-static Document Apparatus (ESDA). ESDA allows impressions left on paper to be enhanced and examined.

David Canter A British scientist (1944–) who is the principle researcher into the 'crime scene analysis' approach to offender profiling. Canter believes that everything that happens at the scene of a crime can scientifically assist in building a psychological profile of the suspect.

GLOSSARY 1

A ready-reference guide to many of the terms used in this book.

Antibody A molecule produced by the body to fight infection and other invading substances.

Antigen A substance (usually a protein) which is recognized and attacked by an antibody.

Anthropology The study of human beings: their structure and evolution, and their culture and organization.

Ballistics The science of projectiles and firearms.

Bertillonage An identification system devised by Alphonse Bertillon, which was based on the idea that each individual's body measurements are different. Investigators could compare details of a suspect with those held on file.

Blood groups A system that was developed by medical researchers to classify blood into groups. The classification allows forensic scientists to say (within varying degrees of certainty) whether or not blood comes from a particular person. The main groups are A, B, AB and O. These may be rhesus positive or negative.

Chromatography A technique used to separate a substance into its components. Components move through the apparatus at different speeds. As each one passes a sensor it produces an electrical charge which can be recorded.

Chromosome A thread-like structure found in the nucleus of a cell. It is made up of DNA and protein arranged in the genes. Genes are the units of inheritance. Each species has characteristic genes and chromosomes.

Cognitive interview A series of memory-enhancing techniques which are increasingly used by police officers to improve the quality and quantity of information obtained from eyewitnesses to crime.

Comparison microscope Two microscopes connected by an arrangement of mirrors allowing two objects to be compared in a single eyepiece. Although developed to help compare bullets, it has a wide range of applications in forensic science.

Criminal type The idea proposed by Cesar Lombroso that physical appearance dictates criminal behaviour. The notion has no scientific standing.

Dactylography This was an early name for what became known as the science of fingerprints.

▼ **Amina Memon, one of the researchers who in 1995 was working on cognitive interview techniques.**

44

Daguerreotype This was a forerunner of the modern photograph. It was necessary for the subjects to stand motionless, often for some minutes. The slightest movement produced a blurred picture. For some portrait photographs, people had their heads clamped by semi-circles of metal behind their necks.

DNA Deoxyribonucleic acid (DNA) is a substance found in the nucleus of a cell. DNA is the genetic code that makes all living things, including human beings, different from one another.

Electron microscope The scanning electron microscope uses a beam of electrons to provide images up to 150,000 times larger than their true size. Images can be viewed on a computer screen or produced as photographs. The procedure is very useful in forensic examination because the sample is not damaged and other tests can follow without fear of contamination (*see* **Exchange principle**).

Emission spectroscopy When a substance burns, it emits light that is typical of the components of the substance. Passing this light through a prism produces a spectrum and allows the components to be analysed. By comparing the spectrum from an unknown substance with data obtained from control samples, the substance can be accurately identified. This technique is known as emission spectroscopy.

▲ **The FBI serology laboratory in Washington DC, USA, is typical of many forensic laboratories. Samples of body fluids taken from suspects or crime scenes are sent here for analysis.**

Exchange principle The idea that 'every contact leaves a trace' is the key feature of almost all forensic science. People leave traces of themselves at the scene of a crime, and these traces attach themselves to clothing, shoes, hands and so on. This applies to criminals and investigators alike. Investigators must take special precautions to ensure they do not contaminate evidence.

Fingerprint classification Most scientific techniques rely on classifying, retrieving and identifying data. Fingerprint classification depends upon standard and identifiable patterns, which occur in one way or another in all fingerprints. The standard patterns are arches, loops, whorls, and deltas (or triangles).

Fingerprints Fingerprint experts use the term 'fingerprints' for the print records made following an arrest. This is to distinguish them from the prints found at a crime scene. These are known as finger-marks.

Forensic scientists Forensic scientists use the most appropriate scientific methods to provide evidence of the guilt or innocence of a person charged with a crime. Forensic laboratories are usually used only for forensic investigation.

Galvanic skin response This is the measurable change in the electrical conductance of the skin. It forms part of the measurements taken by the polygraph, or lie detector.

Identikit A series of line drawings of facial features which in combination produce a likeness of a person described by a witness. Now superseded by Photo-FIT.

Laser A device that sends out a very intense, narrow beam of light which has a very pure colour. The light beam is extremely powerful and can be focused very accurately.

GLOSSARY 2

Mass spectrometry An analysis technique that measures the mass of each component in a compound or mixture. The sample is bombarded with electrons to give charged particles which can be separated by electric and magnetic fields. A trace is recorded on paper and displayed on a computer screen with peaks for each of the components present. The trace is known as a mass spectrum.

Offender profiling An assessment made by a psychologist or psychiatrist of an unidentified person who commits a series of similar crimes. The assessment considers the person's character and possible background, and aims to predict their future behaviour.

Palaeontology The study of life in the geological past.

Pathology The science of diseases that affect the human body.

Photo-FIT A series of photographs of facial features which can be combined together to produce a likeness of a person described by a witness.

Physiology The science of the functions and phenomena of living organisms.

Police The body of people employed in any country to ensure that the citizens keep the peace and obey the law. In many countries there is a tradition of 'civilian' policing, but in some countries the police are part of the army and are government-controlled. In a few countries both forms exist.

Police work covers a multitude of situations. Here are two aspects:

▶ **British police supported by other emergency services beginning the investigation after a terrorist bomb exploded in the financial district of London, Britain, in April 1992.**

▶ **Tokyo police help a young boy find his way through the city streets.**

Polygraph A lie detector that takes measurements of bodily changes such as galvanic skin response (GSR), heart rate and respiration rate. The person analysing the resulting trace makes judgements about whether or not responses to questions are lies or are the truth.

Psychiatry The study and treatment of mental disease.

Psychology The science of the human mind.

Rifling Grooves on the inside of a gun barrel which produce greater accuracy because they cut into the soft metal of the bullet and make it spin. Rifling marks on bullets are unique to the weapon from which the bullets were fired.

Serial crime Repeated criminal activity by the same person.

Trajectory The path made by a bullet after it has been fired from a gun. One part of the study of ballistics is to examine the possible flight paths of bullets. The path depends upon a number of factors which include the type of weapon used, the nature of the ammunition, the distance of the shooter from the target, the weather (for example, the wind speed), and the nature of the material through which the bullet passes.

Trial by ordeal A system used in Europe in the Middle Ages to decide whether a person was guilty or innocent of a crime. People often died in the course of the ordeal.

Ultraviolet light Light-like radiation that is invisible to the human eye. Certain substances shine brightly when bathed in ultraviolet light. Forensic scientists use these substances to reveal marks that would otherwise go undetected.

X-rays Radiation, like light and ultraviolet light, but with a wavelength that is even shorter. X-rays pass through some materials (for example, human flesh) but are reflected or absorbed by others (for example, bone and lead). Photographic images can be produced of the material through which the X-rays do not pass.

GOING FURTHER

Books There are dozens of professional journals and books which are produced for forensic scientists. Here are a few information books for the general reader:
Forensic Science: Selected Topics by T.H. James, Stanley Thornes 1987. This is a book for science teachers explaining how forensic science can be included in science teaching. There are some simple experiments (to be carried out under supervision), some quizzes and even a crossword puzzle.
The Encyclopedia of Forensic Science by Brian Lane, Headline 1992. This book is very comprehensive. Brian Lane is the author of a number of books dealing with crime and criminals. These include *The Murder Guide to Great Britain*, Robinson 1961, and *The Encyclopedia of Serial Killers*, Headline 1992.

The Modern Sherlock Holmes: An Introduction to Forensic Science Today by Judy Williams, Broadside Books 1991. This book is based on a series of BBC Radio programmes broadcast in 1990.
Fiction Patricia D. Cornwell, is the author of a number of books that deal with the work of a Forensic Medical Examiner in the USA. These books are murder mysteries and Cornwell worked in a Medical Examiner's office. Through the character of Dr Kay Scarpetta, Chief Medical Examiner, the author relays a wealth of information about the techniques of forensic science. The books so far are: *Postmortem*, *Body of Evidence*, *Cruel and Unusual*, *All that Remains* and *The Body Farm*. Some scenes in the books are quite graphic. They are not for people who are squeamish.

INDEX